I0420620

Girls' Aggression & Complex Trauma:

Relational Responses

A Series of 13 Blogs

Jane F. Gilgun
Samantha Hirschey
University of Minnesota, Twin Cities, USA

Copyright 2015
by the Center for Advanced Studies in Child Welfare
CASCW, http://cascw.umn.edu

ISBN-13: 978-1517475512

Jane F. Gilgun, PhD, LICSW, is a professor, School of Social Work, University of Minnesota, Twin Cities, USA.

Samantha Hirschey, MSW, LSW, is a research assistant, School of Social Work, University of Minnesota, Twin Cities, USA.

Overview

We wrote this series of blogs on girls' aggression for child welfare social workers, other service providers, educators, and parents. About three million cases of child abuse and neglect are reported each year, and one million cases are substantiated.

These children have experienced complex trauma, which is a series of adversities that are so upsetting that they affect mood, attention, and emotional health and also threaten healthy social, emotional, and neurological development. Children with complex trauma, such as physical and verbal abuse in combination with loss and abandonments, are at risk to behave in aggressive ways. Child welfare social workers, therefore, routinely provide services to children and their families where the children have issues with aggression.

The goal of service to young people who have issues with aggression is to foster their self-compassion that in turn leads to compassion for others. The development of self-compassion arises through experiences of being treated with compassion. This means building relationships with young people. In this blog series, we recommend relational interviews, which are of means encouraging young people to talk about what is important to them. With the establishment of trust, reduction of aggression and increases in prosocial behaviors are possible.

African American young people are over-represented in child welfare caseloads and are also over-represented in cases of aggressive behaviors, suspensions, expulsions, and school dropouts. Child welfare social workers, therefore, negotiate complex issues related to race, ethnicity, gender, trauma, and school policies when they provide services to young clients who behave in aggressive ways.

How child welfare social workers respond to young people can influence the quality of their lives and the quality of the lives of others, such as other students, teachers, siblings, parents, and neighbors. If the aggression is not addressed effectively during the younger years, young people may grow into adults when their aggression may harm their children, other family members, and people in their neighborhoods and communities. Furthermore, there is a well-documented maltreatment to prison pipeline for boys as well as girls. The rates of abuse and neglect among young people in juvenile corrections and prisons are far higher than in the general population.

Child welfare social workers are positioned to affect policies and programs through direct work with young people and with school personnel. They can engage in relational interviews with parents and school staff in order to replace punitive polices with relational and restorative polices.

Purposes of the Blogs

Our purposes are to raise awareness of issues and interventions related to aggression in schools and other settings and to encourage child welfare social workers to take leadership in policies for young people who act out in aggressive ways. Far too often school policies and policies in other settings are punitive rather than restorative and silencing of students rather than inviting them into relationship through dialogue. We spotlight girls' aggression because in national and understandable concerns for boys' aggression, girls are often overlooked.

Our writing of this series of blogs is based on several goals, among them keeping everyone safe and the promotion the optimal development of young people. This includes targets, bystanders, and persons who act in aggressive ways. Our concerns extends to the affects of aggression on school climate and the climate of other settings in which aggression occurs. In schools, aggression affects the safety of students and staff. It also affects learning and the capacities of young people to develop healthy peer relationships. Aggression has similar affects in other settings such as families, neighborhoods, and recreational facilities. Learning and optimal social development take place in settings where people feel safe.

In these blogs, we provide information to child welfare social workers that will guide them to take leadership that promotes the creation of conditions where young people who had been aggressive become prosocial in how they deal with situations that had previously provoked them to behave aggressively. Research shows that effective interventions are based upon relationships of trust. Without trust, interventions are ineffective.

We focus on girls because in recent years public officials have created policies and programs for boys, especially African Americans, while the issues that girls grapple with have received less attention. Concern for boys is understandable given the concern over police shootings of young black men and the well-documented rates of arrest and incarceration of black males. In the focus on males, however, girls have been overlooked despite similar rates of school dropouts and underperformance. In addition, teenage girls are subject to stereotyping that affects their behaviors and life chances such as teen pregnancy. One in four African American girls become pregnant as teens.

Racial stereotyping, expectations, and perceptions of young African American girls as aggressive underachievers are connected to their higher rates of suspensions and expulsions despite data that show they commit infractions at the same rate as other students. Melanie Horton, a 17-year old senior from Upper Darby, Pennsylvania, said, "Day-to-day things—you're bossy, you're aggressive, you're not ladylike—all of us share that experience" (Anderson, 2015, n.p.).

The evidence is in: as a society, we are not responding well to issues that affect the quality of life of young African Americans.

A Program of Activities

In these blogs, we propose a program of activities designed to develop relationships based on trust and supportive communities that create conditions where girls feel respected and understood. In safe and affirming settings, girls and boys want to change their beliefs and behaviors and actually do. Relational interviews can foster supportive communities. Relational interviews are one-on-one or small group interviews whose purposes are to encourage persons to talk about what matters to them with the goal of developing relationships of trust. They are used routinely in community organizing in order to build grassroots coalitions that then work toward a common goal that typically involves changing social policy and practices.

When applied to work with young people who have issues with aggression, relational interviews can lead to the development of a community of support persons to whom young people can turn to in times of stress. For example, girls might seek to talk to trusted others when they think they are about to act in aggressive ways.

The final blogs in this series will show how relational interviews can lead to effective policies and interventions. We will show how relationship-based practice are foundations for group work and other interventions designed for girls with aggressive behaviors. One of the programs we recommend is restorative justice that focuses on the harm aggression does to relationships and on procedures for the repair of relationships.

We will also show how relational interviews can be used to bring about systems changes in schools whose policies are based on punishment, suspensions, and expulsions. The goal is to move schools to relationship-based policies so that young people who behave in aggressive ways will have structure and support that will help them to respond to troublesome situations in prosocial ways. This kind of behavioral change can only happen within supportive settings.

The following are the topics that this blog series covers.

Much is at stake when young people behave in aggressive ways. We hope that this series of blogs contributes to an increased capacity for child welfare social workers to provide leadership in schools, families, and other settings where young people live their lives.

References

Anderson, Melinda D. (2015). Black girls should matter, too. The Atlantic, May 11. http://www.theatlantic.com/education/archive/2015/05/black-girls-should-matter-too/392879/

Dupper, David R., Matthew T. Theriot, and Sarah W. Craun (2009). Reducing out of school suspensions: Practice guidelines for school social workers. Children & Schools, 31(1), 6-14.

Gilgun, Jane F. (2011). Jacinta's lament: Happy father's day, dad. Amazon.

Gonzalez, T. (2012). Keeping kids in schools: Restorative justice, punitive discipline, and the school to prison pipeline. Journal of Law and Education, 41(2), 281-235.

Gilbert, R., Widom, C. S., Browne, K., Fergusson, D., Webb, E. & Janson, S. (2009). Burden and consequences of child maltreatment in high-income countries. Lancet, 373(9657), 68–81.

Mullet, Judy Hostetler (2014). Restorative discipline: From getting even to getting well. Children & Schools, 36 (3), 157-162.

Ruch, Gillian (2005). Relationship practice and reflective practice: Holistic approaches to contemporary child care social work. Child and Family Social Work, 10, 111-123.

Ruch, Gillian, Danielle Turney and Adrian Ward (Eds.) (2010). Relationship-based social work: Getting to the heart of practice. London: Jessica Kingsley.

Teasley, Martell L. (2014) Shifting from zero tolerance to restorative justice in schools. Children and Schools 36 (3), 131-133.

Blog 1
Worthlessness and Self-Compassion

Young people who have experienced abuse and neglect often feel worthless, unlovable, and unworthy of respect. Professionals often tell them, "It's not your fault." This might provide temporary relief, but the negative beliefs are deeply embedded. They don't go away without the help of adults who provide safe havens where young people can grapple with the meanings the maltreatment has for them.

Safe havens are settings where young people can experience themselves as loveable and worthy of love and respect. Through these experiences, they develop self-compassion and compassion for others. In our experience, adults often ignore young people's sense of worthlessness. They may not know how to deal with it, or they may not realize how a sense of worthlessness affects young people.

Worthlessness

Persons who have experienced abuse and neglect often believe something about themselves caused the maltreatment. They may conclude that they are worthless, unlovable, and unworthy of respect and become reactive to perceived slights. In response, many become aggressive physically, verbally, or sexually. Aggression gives temporary relief and temporary restoration of their sense of worth and pride. Some withdraw and isolate to avoid further hurt. Others become self-destructive, seeking to soothe their hurt through cutting, sniffing solvents, and using drugs and alcohol.

When young people feel safe and respected, their behaviors are prosocial and cooperative. Any work with young people, therefore, requires that adults build relationships of trust with them. The best scenario is when the social setting, such as schools and families, are circles of trust and safe havens where young people can work on the issues connected to their aggression.

Self-Compassion

Persons who have histories of secure attachments, beginning in infancy with their parents and others and continuing over the life course have naturally occurring self-compassion. Self-compassion is positive regard for the self as worthy of respect and love during good times and times of challenge.

Persons who have self-compassion accept themselves as imperfect, view their experiences as part of the human condition, and allow themselves to experience painful thoughts and feelings, knowing that emotions have a natural flow when persons allow themselves to experience them. They do not ruminate or behave destructively but engage in processes that lead to a working through of painful emotions. They hold themselves accountable for any hurt they cause and seek to repair damage to relationship with others. Self-compassion begins when young people experience compassion from others.

If persons have self-compassion, they have compassion for others. Compassion is associated with loving kindness, which they extend toward their own imperfections and failures and those of others. Their compassion for others and themselves flows from an inner sense of dignity and self-worth.

Research shows that low self-compassion is associated with harsh experiences, usually in childhood and sometimes later in life, and the absence of relationships with others that provide safe havens where individuals can work through the effects of these experiences. Child abuse and neglect, rape, separations and losses, and other adverse and traumatic events are examples of harsh experiences. Girls with child protection involvement have lower self-compassion than girls who are not under the care of child protection. Research shows that they are more likely to engage in aggressive behaviors and to be targets of aggression than girls without child protection involvement. Research shows self-compassion can be increased through positive life experiences based on relationships of trust.

Self-Compassion and Trusting Relationships

When young people participate in interventions based on relationships of trust, they may develop self-compassion. Supportive, respectful, and structured social settings help persons develop and maintain self-compassion and compassion for others.

Because of the importance of supportive social settings, child protection workers who are effective in school settings not only advocate for relationship-based interventions but they also work to bring about systems changes.

Summary

In summary, the goals of work with young people with aggressive behaviors are to stop the aggression and foster prosocial behaviors through building relationships of trust. Through circles of trust, young people develop compassion for self and others. These principles underlie effective interventions. Such interventions are difficult to develop and implement in many schools and other settings. Today's blog lays out the best case scenario, the ideal outcome. We know that in real-world situations, these principles are part of a vision and may not be difficult to achieve.

Questions To Consider

As you think about the blog, we wonder what you think of some of the ideas that we presented. What, for example, do you think we left out? Was there anything in this blog that helped you think more deeply about your cases? We hope you consider the following questions.

* What kinds of behaviors do you see in your caseload that indicate that service users feel unloved, unlovable, disrespected, and worthless?
* How do you deal with the times you feel unloved, unlovable, disrespected, and worthless?
* Do you think self-compassion is an issue for young people and their families who are in your caseload? Why or why not?
* Think of times when you have had self-compassion. What is self-compassion like for you?

References

Gilgun, Jane F. (2006). Children and adolescents with problematic sexual behaviors: Lessons from research on resilience. In Robert Longo & Dave Prescott (Eds.), Current perspectives on working with sexually aggressive youth and youth with sexual behavior problems (pp. 383-394). Holyoke, MA: Neari Press.

Gilgun, Jane F., & Laura S. Abrams (2005). Gendered adaptations, resilience, and the perpetration of violence. In Michael Ungar (Ed.), Handbook for working with children and Youth: Pathways to resilience across cultures and context (pp. 57-70). Toronto: University of Toronto Press.

Gilgun, Jane F., Danette Jones, & Kay Rice. (2005). Emotional expressiveness as an indicator of progress in treatment. In Martin C. Calder (Ed.), Emerging approaches to work with children and young people who sexually abuse (pp. 231-244). Dorset, England: Russell House.

Gilgun, Jane F. (2011). Children with serious conduct issues: A case study, a NEATS assessment, and case planning. Amazon Kindle.

Neff, K.D. (2003). Self-compassion: An alternative conceptualization of a healthy attitude toward oneself. Self and Identity, 2, 85–102.

Neff, K. D., Kirkpatrick, K. L., & Rude, S. S. (2007). Self-compassion and adaptive psychological functioning. Journal of Research in Personality, 41, 139–154.

Neff, K. D. & McGehee, P. (2010). Self-compassion and psychological resilience among adolescents and young adults. Self and Identify, 9(3), 225–240.

Perepletchikova, F. & Kaufman, J. (2010, October). Emotional and behavioral sequelae of childhood maltreatment. Current Opinion in Pediatrics, 22(5), 610–615.

Promoting Safe, Stable and Nurturing Relationships: A Strategic Direction for Child Maltreatment Prevention Us Centers for Disease Control and Prevention website:http://www.cdc.gov/ViolencePrevention/pdf/CM_Strategic_Direction--OnePager-a.pdf.

Tanakaa, Masako, Christine Wekerle, Mary Lou Schmuck, Angela Paglia-Boak, & the MAP research team (2011). The linkages among childhood maltreatment, adolescent mental health, and self-compassion in child welfare adolescents. Child Abuse & Neglect (35), 887–898.

Thompson, Brian L. & Jennifer Waltz (2008). Self-compassion and PTSD symptom severity. Journal of Traumatic Stress, 21(6), 556–558.

Blog 2
Girls' Aggression: An Overview

Girls' aggression is a growing concern in families, schools, and communities. Aggression is disregard for the well-being of others that results in physical, emotional, and psychological injury. For persons who commit aggression, their behaviors are logical, normal, and often necessary for them to maintain their self-respect and the respect of others. Others experience their acts as harmful and even dangerous. Any concerns individuals have for the harm their aggression causes arise after the fact. At the time individuals act, they are thinking only of consequences they believe are beneficial for themselves and sometimes for others. For targets of the aggression and for most other people, these same acts are not only harmful but must be stopped.

These blogs are based upon interviews with knowledgeable professionals, on published research and theory, and on the authors' professional and research experiences. We spotlight girls' relational aggression, which is a non-contact form of aggression that is as harmful as physical aggression but that adults often dismiss as harmless.

Persons who commit relational aggression intend to harm social standings and reputations and cause breakdowns in the relationships that targeted persons, usually other girls, have with others. It alters the perceptions of girls who are targeted and affects their social standing. Acts of relational aggression include gossiping, exclusion, ignoring, threatening to withdraw or withdrawing friendship or social acceptance, misrepresentations through innuendo, distortions, or lies, and spreading rumors so that others will distance themselves from or reject targets.

Relational aggression can take place in real time or through postings on the internet and other social media. Adults often ignore this kind of aggression if they notice it at all. They believe that young people will work it out themselves. They can, when all parties are willing and when there is equality in power and social status. If there is an imbalance of power, the dominant person can inflict serious emotional and damage to the targeted persons' social standing and sense of self. For children and young people, schools are settings where many of these acts of aggression occur. Child welfare social workers often are called into schools to deal with these issues.

Aggression and Relationships

Typically, the kinds of aggression that come to the attention of school authorities are physical, either physical fighting as in punching, kicking, and hair-pulling or throwing objects such as desks, chairs, and computers. Less overt forms of aggression include gossip, misrepresentation of others, and social exclusion. Authorities seek to end physical aggression while other forms may be ignored or dismissed as harmless.

Often the first response of school authorities is to isolate perpetrators, insist that they show remorse, and stop the behaviors. When young people do not comply, authorities often implement zero tolerance policies of suspension and expulsion. This solves the immediate problem, but it is a kind of "geographic cure," where the young people continue to behave in physically aggressive ways in new settings. Furthermore, expulsion does nothing to help the young people learn prosocial ways of dealing with difficult situations.

Expulsions also may destabilize young people so that their use of aggression increases and becomes ingrained. Finally, expulsion models to young people ineffective ways of dealing with troublesome situations. A great deal of research shows the ineffectiveness of zero tolerance policies. There is wide-spread concern that zero tolerance is not only ineffective but punitive, too.

In the absence of effective interventions, girls are unlikely to outgrow their behaviors but will continue to harm others and their own life chances. They could be set up for life-long trajectories of aggression that not only will affect them but will affect their relationship with others including their own children, families, and communities.

Child welfare social workers are routinely involved in situations where children and young people engage in aggressive behaviors. Early, effective intervention will help children and young people to develop prosocial ways of handling troublesome situations and so open up possibilities for them to lead fulfilling lives and to contribute to the social good. If interventions are not effective, beliefs about aggression become embedded in how young people think and become habits of mind and action that are encoded in brain circuits.

Summary

In summary, girls' aggression is a growing concern. Child welfare social workers routinely engage in situations where girls in their caseloads have acted out aggressively. Suspensions and expulsions are geographic cures that not only don't work but are harmful. This series of blogs view girls' aggression as a relational issue, signaling a breakdown in capacities for relationships based on trust. Effective responses to girls' aggression are based upon building relationships of trust.

Questions To Consider

As you think about the blog, we wonder what you think of some of the ideas that we presented. What, for example, do you think we left out? Was there anything in this blog that helped you think more deeply about your cases? We hope you consider the following questions.

* What do you think of the idea that aggression creates mistrust?

* What kinds of school policies toward aggression do you have experience with?

* How effective are they?

* Have you every heard of relational aggression?

* If no, does this discussion help you to identify these behaviors in the children and families in your caseload?

*If yes, what are some examples of

* the behaviors you've seen,

* the effects of these behaviors,

* and the responses of adults to these behaviors?

References

Tanakaa, Masako, Christine Wekerle Mary Lou Schmuck, Angela Paglia-Boak, & the MAP research team (2011). The linkages among childhood maltreatment, adolescent mental health, and self-compassion in child welfare adolescents. Child Abuse & Neglect (35), 887–898

Teasley, Martell L. (2014) Shifting from zero tolerance to restorative justice in schools. Children and Schools 36 (3), 131-133.

Tesh, Miki & Joy Learman & Rose M. Pulliam (2015). Mindful self-compassion: Strategies for survivors of intimate partner abuse. Mindfulness, 6, 192–201.

Blog 3
Types of Aggression:
Instrumental and Reactive

Persons who commit aggressive acts base their behaviors on widely-held beliefs and practices. Often their families, communities, and mass media promote the kinds of aggression that they commit. Children and their families who become clients in child welfare agencies often are survivors of physical abuse and other forms of family violence including physical and verbal abuse between the adults in their families. Witnessing violence and being targets of violence are well-established risks for perpetrating aggressive behaviors. These risks can be managed when survivors have had relationships with others who helped them to work through the effects and meanings of the aggression that they have witnessed and experienced.

Beliefs and practices that young people absorb in families and communities are reinforced through mass media. Many films, for example, glorify aggression in the name of vengeance and setting things right. Vengeance is presented as a good thing, necessary to make things right and applauded for doing so. It is no coincidence that young people who act in aggressive ways often believe they are setting things right and expect congratulations for doing so.

Targets of aggression, bystanders, friends, and professionals, however, have other points of view and want the behaviors to stop. They also may want perpetrators to be accountable and to apologize. Professionals often have difficulty shifting perspectives in order to connect to and understand the points of view of persons who act in aggressive ways. Starting where clients are is a basic social work principle. Effective practice with persons who commit aggressive acts begins with understanding the meanings of aggression, both to themselves and to the persons who are their clients.

Types of Aggression

Aggression can be of two broad types: instrumental and reactive.

Instrumental Aggression

Instrumental aggression is an unprovoked, purposeful and non-emotional means of achieving dominance over others and getting what you want at the expense of others. In social settings such as schools, it often is mean to increase popularity among peers.

Bullying is often instrumental in nature, and there are overlaps between aggression and bullying. The purpose of bullying is to display power and dominance over others and often to have fun. Sometimes bullies and the bullied have relationships with others, such as in sibling bullying, but in other settings such as schools, bullies and the bullied do not have social relationships.

Girls' aggression may be based on desires to dominate and display power and can be a form of bullying. However, in much of girls' aggression, including relational, verbal, sexual, and physical, relationships are at issue. Therefore, in understanding girls' aggression—as well as boys—questions about how relationships are in play may help in the development of effective responses.

Persons who engage in instrumental aggression often experience their aggressive behaviors as fun, and they may not realize that their behaviors not only may cause long-term harm to targets but also create a climate of mistrust and fear that interferes with learning, with social and emotional development, and with the development of healthy peer relationships.

Reactive Aggression

Reactive aggression stems from perceived or actual threats. The individuals believe that in particular situations something important is at stake, and they must respond in order to maintain self-respect and the respect of at least some others. They may experience the threat as a physical sensation, something like electricity that shoots through their bodies. They go into automatic and behave in ways that have become ingrained. They also may go into dysregulated states, where flight or fight responses are activated and the thinking part of their brains shuts down. They may not realize the effects of their behaviors on others and on the social climates in which their behaviors take place.

Like instrumental aggression, commonly-held beliefs and practice have a part to play in reactive aggression. Many young people experience complex trauma but do not act in aggressive ways. The differences between those who act out aggressively and those who do not appear to be beliefs. Persons who have experienced trauma and who do not act out in aggressive ways have a history of secure attachments with parents and others, have grown up in prosocial environments where aggression is not valued and prosociality is, and where they have learned that aggression hurts others. They may have some pro-aggression beliefs, but their other positive experiences have helped them to develop capacities for managing their aggression.

Reactive Aggression and Child Welfare Social Work

Reactive aggression is common in children who have experienced complex trauma, which is a series of difficult life events that interfere with the development of trust and thus the building of healthy relationships. Complex trauma also affects emotional and social development, capacities for maintaining focus and attention, and creates fears about the self as worthy of love and respect. Each year, about three million children are reported as abused and neglected, and one million of these reports are substantiated. Therefore, uncounted numbers of young people have experienced complex trauma. While many of them do not commit acts of aggression, many do. Aggression, then, is a core issue in child welfare practice.

When young people have experienced complex trauma, they may misread social cues and attribute hostile intent where none exists. These perceptions lead to fears of rejection and ridicule from others. They may become hypervigilant and primed for defending themselves when they are in classrooms, lunchrooms, and other social situations. Misattributions of social cues are called deficits in social information processing.

Summary

In summary, aggression has many sources. In this blog, we have discussed instrumental and reactive aggression. It is important for child welfare social workers to understand both types in order to tailor their responses to individual children and their situations. When the aggression is primarily reactive, trauma-specific work is called for. If the aggression is instrumental, less time may be needed to deal with trauma. In both types, however, careful work will help young people to gradually change the beliefs that underlie both types of aggression are necessary.

In addition, in some types of aggression, the young people have not experienced complex trauma that is typical in child welfare caseloads. Differential assessment is important to identify the possible factors that feed the aggressive behaviors.

Questions To Consider

What, for example, do you think we left out? Was there anything in this blog that helped you think more deeply about your cases? As you think about the blog, we wonder whether you have had experiences with relational aggression. We hope you consider the following questions.

* Is it useful for you to know that there are two broad types of aggression: Reactive and instrumental?
* How might know this be helpful or not helpful to you in your work?
* If you know a young person's aggression behaviors are mostly reactive in nature, does it make sense to wonder

whether this reactivity is learned behavior, related to past trauma, or a combination? Please explain your answer.

* Have you ever experienced a desire for revenge?

* Whatever your response, we encourage you to think about why or why not.

* Have you seen instances where young people behave in aggressive ways and have not experienced complex trauma?

* What have you seen as sources of their aggression?

References

Crick, N. R. (1997) Engagement in gender normative versus nonnormative forms of aggression: Links to social-psychological adjustment. Developmental Psychology, 33(4), 610-617.

Crick, N.R. & Grotpeter, J.K. (1995). Relational aggression, gender, and social-psychological adjustment. Child Development, 66 (3), 710-722.

Dailey, A. L., Frey, A. J., & Walker, H. M. (2015). Relational aggression in school settings: Definition, development, strategies and implications. Children & Schools. 37(2). 79-88.

Espelage, D. L., Basile, K. C. & Hamburger, M.E. (2012) Bullying perpetration and subsequent sexual violence perpetration among middle school students. Society for Adolescent Health and Medicine, 50 (1), 60-65.

Lingras, K. A. (2012). For better or worse? A developmental perspective on the role of executive function in relational aggression: A dissertation submitted to the faculty of the graduate school of the University of Minnesota. University of Minnesota Libraries Digital Conservancy.

Shields, A. & Cicchetti, D. (1998). Reactive aggression among maltreated children: The contributions of attention and emotion dysregulation. Journal of Clinical Child Psychology, 27(4), 381-395.

Tisak, M.S., Wichorek, M.G. & Tisak, J. (2011). Relation between exposure to and consequences of aggression: U.S. national sample of adolescents. Journal of School Violence. 10(4), 355-373.

Winlow, Simon & Steve Hall (2009). Retaliate first: Memory, humiliation and male violence. Crime, Media, Culture, 5, 285-304.

Blog 4
Types of Aggression:
Non-Contact and Contact Aggression

Instrumental and reactive aggression can be non-contact or contact behaviors. In non-contact aggression, individuals use words and non-verbal expressions such as gestures and facial expressions that harm others. In contact aggression, individuals have bodily contact that can be in the forms of hair-pulling, kicking, and punching and also can involve contact with sexual body parts. Both contact and non-contact types of aggression cause psychological distress and may be sources of trauma that has long-term harmful effects.

Contact and non-contact aggression affect relationships in that they cause breakdowns in trust or signal breakdowns in trust. They affect the sense of safety of others who are part of the social setting.

Relational Aggression

As the name implies, relational aggression damages relationships, affects reputations, and social standing, and threatens the sense of self as lovable and worthy of dignity and respect. It is non-contact aggression that includes gossiping, exclusion, ignoring, threatening to withdraw or withdrawing friendship or social acceptance in order to control and hurt the victim, and spreading rumors about the victim so that others will reject her. Relational aggression may be overt, such as teasing, or more subtle, such as not inviting someone to a social gathering. Relational aggression is common in schools and social groups where young people congregate.

The intention of relational aggression is to exclude others from social groups. Relational aggression can occur in real time or through the internet, such as posting unkind comments or unflattering or embarrassing photographs. It typically is instrumental in nature, done for a laugh with no intent to harm, but sometimes individuals use it when they perceive others as threatening them in some way. In such circumstances, relational aggression is reactive, that is in response to perceived or actual threats.

A situation that often gives rise to instrumental relational aggression is when young people are new to a school or other setting. Some others may perceive them as vulnerable because they do not yet have supportive friendships. They take advantage of this situational vulnerability and act in ways that exclude the new persons, often in their own minds, for the fun of it.

Girls in child welfare caseloads may use relational aggression but relational aggression is also common among girls who are not identified as highly stressed and traumatized. When stress and trauma are not at issue in relational aggression, educational programs might help the young people understand that they hurt others by their behaviors. When stress and trauma are at issue, the interventions may require long-term, in-depth work that we will discuss in later blogs.

Relational aggression may progress to verbal, physical, and sexual aggression. School officials and treatment professionals state that girls who have experienced complex trauma are at risk for this kind of acceleration. Early, effective intervention is called for.

Verbal Aggression

Verbal aggression consists of name-calling, swearing, and threats to harm. Verbal aggression can occur in real time or through internet postings. People who engage in verbal aggression often view the situations in which they aggress as somehow threatening to them, either physically or in terms of their own psychological safety and sense of self-worth. They react in aggressive ways in order to protect themselves and not to exclude others. Therefore their behaviors can be considered acts of reactive aggression.

Sometimes verbal aggression is an attempt to control and dominate others, or even as a way of "getting a rise out of someone," and thus to have "fun" at the expense of others. Under these conditions, verbal aggression is instrumental. The situation is not threatening to aggressors but is one conducive to dominating and even intimidating others.

It can be difficult to distinguish between relational aggression and verbal aggression, as there is overlap. Relational aggression is intended to put a wedge between targets and their relationships with others while verbal aggression is meant to hurt and control others or to show defiance and lack of fear of authority figures. The language young people may use in verbal aggression is not pretty.

A case example. Queenie, 13, physically attacked the school principal while shouting, "I don't fucking care who you are. You're going to get it. I'll fight you right back. I'm not fucking kissing anybody's ass." Such behaviors indicate not only the possibility of complex trauma but long-term exposure to many different types of aggression that persons important to Queenie view as normal, necessary, and valued. A simple reprimand will not get at the sources of Queenie's actions. Queenie requires trusting relationships where she will gradually value herself and through valuing herself value others. In other words, a long-term goal for young people like Queenie is to develop self-compassion that leads to compassion for others. This is no simple task. The final blogs in this series will suggest ways of achieving this goal.

Physical Aggression

Hitting, pushing, kicking, biting, and hair pulling are all forms of physical aggression. Physical aggression can either be moderate or severe. Examples of moderate physical aggression are pushing or slapping, while severe forms of physical violence include stabbings, shootings, and wildings, where are groups of people severely beat someone to death or close to death. As the example of Queenie shows, verbal and physical aggression may go together.

Sexual Aggression

Sexual aggression includes non-contact forms such as sexual harassment, verbal innuendo, sexualized looks, and stalking and contact such as butt slapping, grabbing genitals or breasts, and forcible penetration such as rape and sodomy. Other common forms of sexual aggression among school age young people are the sharing of sexual photographs, text messages, and notes, pulling down another person's clothing, saying someone is gay or lesbian, blocking or cornering someone that conveys sexually aggressive intent, and spreading sexual rumors.

Summary

As this blog shows, there are many types of aggression. Each type harms other people and can affect learning, social and emotional development, and the development of healthy peer relationships. Children and young people in child welfare caseloads are at high risk to behave in aggressive ways because they have experienced complex trauma and others rarely have helped them work through its effects. Early, effective interventions can result in the development of prosocial behaviors in situations that previously led to aggression. Effective interventions contribute to classroom safety and school safety in general, increased learning, and increased social and emotional development. Early, effective intervention can have beneficial effects in other social settings as well, such as families, neighborhoods, and recreational facilities.

Questions To Consider

As you think about the blog, we wonder whether you have had experiences with relational aggression. What, for example, do you think we left out? Was there anything in this blog that helped you think more deeply about your cases? We hope you consider the following questions.

* Have you had young people in your caseload who behave as Queenie does?

* What were their families like?

* How did school personnel respond?

* What were the outcomes of the cases?

* Sexual aggression is common in schools. Have you had young people in your caseload who have sexual behavior issues?

* What resources were available to these young people?

* What factors are associated with the development of sexual behavior issues in the young people with whom you have worked?

* Have you seen instances where young people behave in aggressive ways and have not experienced complex trauma?

* What have you seen as sources of their aggression?

* How important do you think differential assessment is

* In doing differential assessments, what factors might be important to consider?

* Do you think young people with complex trauma also have personal and social attributes that might be mobilized in helping them deal with the sources of their aggressive behaviors?

References

Crick, N. R. (1997) Engagement in gender normative versus nonnormative forms of aggression: Links to social-psychological adjustment. Developmental Psychology, 33(4), 610-617.

Crick, N.R. & Grotpeter, J.K. (1995). Relational aggression, gender, and social-psychological adjustment. Child Development, 66 (3), 710-722.

Dailey, A. L., Frey, A. J., & Walker, H. M. (2015). Relational aggression in school settings: Definition, development, strategies and implications. Children & Schools. 37(2). 79-88.

Espelage, D. L., Basile, K. C. & Hamburger, M.E. (2012) Bullying perpetration and subsequent sexual violence perpetration among middle school students. Society for Adolescent Health and Medicine, 50 (1), 60-65.

Lingras, K. A. (2012). For better or worse? A developmental perspective on the role of executive function in relational aggression: A dissertation submitted to the faculty of the graduate school of the University of Minnesota. University of Minnesota Libraries Digital Conservancy.

Shields, A. & Cicchetti, D. (1998). Reactive aggression among maltreated children: The contributions of attention and emotion dysregulation. Journal of Clinical Child Psychology, 27(4), 381-395.

Tisak, M.S., Wichorek, M.G. & Tisak, J. (2011). Relation between exposure to and consequences of aggression: U.S. national sample of adolescents. Journal of School Violence. 10(4), 355-373.

Winlow, Simon & Steve Hall (2009). Retaliate first: Memory, humiliation and male violence. Crime, Media, Culture, 5, 285-304.

Girls' Relational Aggression:
Targets of the Aggression

Girls' relational aggression is behavior intended to damage the relationships of others. As stated earlier, relational aggression includes teasing, gossiping, ostracism, threatening to withdraw or directly withdrawing friendship or social acceptance, misrepresenting others, and spreading rumors. Some relational aggression arises from competition over boys.

Acts of relational aggression are usually not blatant and are thus more difficult to identify than overt, physical aggression. Parents should be mindful that relational aggression is not isolated to peer relationships, but also occurs between siblings. Displays of relational aggression at home may include: excluding siblings from activities, name-calling, and covering one's ears to signal ignoring, which is behavior particularly seen among younger children. Sibling RA is typically extended from elder to younger siblings, and research indicates that younger siblings who are victimized by RA at home are then relationally aggressive towards peers elsewhere.

Relational aggression can be overt or covert. Often targets of relational aggression know who the perpetrators are. This is overt relational aggression that may come in the form of direct statements and nonverbal communication such as facial expression, hand movements, and social exclusion, as in not inviting someone to join a social activity. At other times, relational aggression is covert, where targets don't know the sources of the aggression. Leaving hurtful anonymous notes or comments on the internet, lobbying friends to exclude someone, or starting rumors are examples of covert relational aggression. Individuals may engage in covert aggression to avoid counter-aggression and to avoid being known as a person who would seek to harm others.

Adolescence and Effects of Relational Aggression

Adolescence is a time of physical changes, growing self and social awareness, and school transitions, which can leave younger individuals feeling insecure and vulnerable, even without being targets of relational aggression. Leadbetter (2010) said that in adolescence, "Peer group membership is central to the affirmation of identity and regulation of self esteem and fuels a sense of urgency to be included in peer relationships (p. 589)." Being targeted for relational aggression can have negative long-term affects on relationships, identity, and self-worth.

According to Dailey, Frey and Walker (2015), when adolescents experience relational aggression, they are risk for experiencing

> (a) future peer rejection, (b) social maladjustment, such as friendship problems, (c) internalizing problems in the forms of isolation and loneliness as well as depression, (d) anxiety problems, and (e) school avoidance, and poor academic performance, impaired school adjustment, and ultimately school failure and dropout (p. 79).

In severe cases, survivors of relational aggression may seek protection through gang membership and engage in retaliatory and reactive aggression, suicidal thoughts, and suicide.

Many young people who are targets of relational aggression have families and friends who are supportive and provide the safety and security necessary to work through the effects of social exclusion and rejection. Some may be students in schools or social settings that have procedures that respond effectively in cases of relational aggression. Targets of the aggression have the trusting relationship that provide the support required to cope with the aggression without being aggressive themselves. Their lack of reactance gives no reinforcement to the aggressive behaviors. Young people who engage in aggressive behaviors and who have relationships of trust are responded to authoritatively. Adults seek to understand them and form relationships with them while being clear that they must not harm others.

Some young people confide in parents and others but the help that others offer is insufficient. It could be that the young people perceive the wider social context as unsympathetic and indifferent to their hurt. Indeed, in many instances, other people don't understand their suffering and are dismissive. Even when parents are empathic, their efforts may be insufficient to affect how young people perceive themselves and their social status. Their hurt and the consequences of the hurt can be deep and lasting.

Often, young people who are targets of relational aggression are too ashamed to tell anyone about how their peers treat them. Some want to maintain an image of being popular with peers and don't want to disappoint their parents and others who care about them. They isolate themselves from others and may ruminate about their worthlessness and how they deserve to be treated badly. Often relationally aggressive peers tell them they are worthless.

There is mounting evidence that when young people commit suicide other children not only have excluded them from social groups but they tell them they are worthless and sometimes encourage them to commit suicide. In such cases relational aggression goes beyond the desire to harm another person's relationships. It becomes a form of aggression that is life-threatening. Under these conditions, young people are unable to handle relational aggression on their own. Aggressors must stop. Often they think they are having fun and don't anticipate the impact of another young person's suicide on them. Survivors require safety, reassurance, and opportunities to work through what the aggression means to them.

Many people assume that targets of relational aggression are young people who already are vulnerable and something about them provokes the aggression of others. Young people can and do harass and bully children who appear different to them, such as having facial deformities or other physical differences. In these instances, this is not relational aggression but a form of verbal aggression to which adults must respond to in order to limit the damage such abuse causes.

Targets of relational aggression may be young people who are new to social settings. Other girls may want to assert power and control, which gives them pleasure, by excluding these girls. After a period of time, if the targets are able to withstand the aggression, they are accepted into the social group and the aggression stops. How often this happens is unknown.

Targets of relational aggression may also be girls who have many social assets, such as physical attractiveness, intelligence, good grades, popularity, and athleticism. Relational aggression toward them may arise because their attributes and accomplishments activate insecurities and fears of worthless in others, who rather than deal with their insecurities, take them out on others.

Relational aggression often occurs within the context of inconsistent friendships, where the most popular or well-liked member of a social group can change day-to-day, depending on the attitudes of other group members. In more severe cases, a victim of relational aggression is completely ostracized from their friendship group, excluded from all areas of prior social engagement, such as the lunch table, sports, games, and not being invited to parties.

Still other targets of relational aggression appear to be taking something away from the aggressor, such as a boyfriend or social standing. In such situations, girls who feel something has been taken from them or respond in ways they intend to damage the girls they perceive as competitors.

Aside from a desire for social dominance, relational aggression may also stem from jealousy and revenge. For girls in middle and high school, the emergence into dating relationships and sexual activity may also instigate gossip, rumors, and social exclusion. Prejudice against racial groups, social class, and sexual orientation and expression may also trigger acts of relational aggression. The advancement of internet and personal cell phone use, as well as social media, has expanded the arenas for where relational aggression occurs. Facebook and text messaging has increased the reach of humiliating tactics against targets, such as the viral sharing of photographs and spread of malicious messages.

Summary

Relational aggression is a serious problem in schools and other social settings. It is important to understand the various forms of relational aggression and its effects on targets and others in the setting. Young people can cope with the effects of relational aggression if adults and peers provide them with opportunities to talk through the meanings and affects of the aggression and the young people are assured that they are worthwhile human beings and that the aggressors are behaving in unkind and unfair ways.

Questions to Consider

As you think about the blog, we wonder how you are responding to the ideas we presented. What, for example, do you think we left out? Was there anything in this blog that helped you think more deeply about your cases?

We hope you consider the following questions.

* Have you ever witnessed relational aggression?
* What do you think was going on with aggressors?
* Were there bystanders who encouraged the aggressors?
What did they do?
What did you do?
* Did racial stereotyping have a part to play?
* Have you ever been the target of relational aggression?
* What effect did this have on you?
* Did anyone encourage the aggressors? What did they do? What did you do?
* Did racial stereotyping have a part to play?
* Did you talk to anyone about being a target of relational aggression?
* Did talking help?

* Have you ever performed acts of relational aggression?

* What did you tell yourself you were doing?

* How did other people respond to your relational aggression?

* Did racial stereotyping have a part to play?

* Did you talk to anyone about being your relational aggression?

* Did talking help?

* There have been many well-publicized stories in the media about young people who commit suicide in response to bullying. Can you see connections between bullying and relational aggression?

References

Crick, N. R. (1997) Engagement in gender normative versus nonnormative forms of aggression: Links to social-psychological adjustment. Developmental Psychology, 33(4), 610-617.

Crick, N.R. & Grotpeter, J.K. (1995). Relational aggression, gender, and social-psychological adjustment. Child Development, 66 (3), 710-722.

Dailey, A. L., Frey, A. J., & Walker, H. M. (2015). Relational aggression in school settings: Definition, development, strategies and implications. Children & Schools. 37(2). 79-88.

Hammel, L. R. (2008). Bouncing back after bullying: The resiliency of female victims of relational aggression mid-western educational researcher. 21(2), 3-14.

Leadbetter, B. (2010). Can we see it? Can we stop it? Lessons learned from community-university research collaborations about relational aggression. School Psychology Review. 39(4). pp. 588-593.

Pronk, R.E. & Zimmer-Gembeck, M.J. (2010) It's "mean," but what does it mean to adolescents? Relational aggression described by victims, aggressors, and their peers. Journal of Adolescent Research. 25(2) 175-204

Blog 6

Relational Aggression:
Girls who Perpetrate

In blog 5, we discussed definitions, the experiences of survivors of relational aggression, and the long-term developmental risks of these behaviors for survivors. In this blog, we discuss the meanings of relational aggression to perpetrators. We also show how aggression is an executive function issue, meaning that girls may not understand the consequences of their behaviors, disregard commonly-held rules of conduct, and may have serious issues with self-regulation.

Why Girls Engage in Relational Aggression

Girls engage in relational aggression for many different reasons. Girls' aggression is typically reactive, rather than instrumental, and is often more verbal than physical. Girls are also more likely than boys to be aggressive toward those with whom they have close relationships, such as friends, siblings, and other family members.

When relational aggression is instrumental, one or more girls may have taken a dislike to another and use relational aggression to keep her away from them. They may not understand the consequences of their exclusion of other girls.

Relational aggression can be based on desires for affiliation, power, and status. Other motivations for relational aggression include creating excitement to elevate mood, group inclusion, jealousy, revenge, and self-protection.

Relational aggression may also stem from viewing others with contempt because of their perceived worthlessness that originate in widely-held attitudes and prejudices about classes of people based on their social attributes. Adults concerned about girls' aggression, therefore, will be effective to the extent that they can create conditions where girls explore their beliefs related to race and ethnicity, gender, sexual orientation and identity, and any other issue and stereotypes that underlie their aggression. Girls' aggression also may experience racism where they receive unfair treatment and biases about their attributes. Girls' aggression may stem from their own experiences of hurt, sense of worthlessness, and beliefs about their own lovability (Christa Nelson, personal communication, May 2015).

Relational aggression is rooted sensitive, private issues that girls may be reluctant to share. Adults who can effectively lead girls through an examination and letting go of these beliefs and hurts would have capacities for creating a sense of safety, or safe havens. Safe havens are based upon relationships of trust. Blog 10 will provide guidelines for developing trusting relationships. In this blog, we continue do further explorations of relational aggression.

Social Status

Perpetrators of relational aggression may be of high or low status. High status individuals possess traits considered positive by others, whereas low status individuals possess traits considered negative or socially bothersome. Schools are a frequent setting for relational aggression and high-status perpetrators, such as those who are popular, skilled, and competitive, may go unnoticed by staff if they possess academic or athletic strengths.

High status perpetrators whose positive traits may be highlighted in the classroom or on sports teams may be given the benefit of the doubt by teachers, coaches and parents. This propensity to give benefit of the doubt fuels a common misconception by adults that relational aggression is a typical adolescent behavior that doesn't require intervention. Another common misperception is that all bullies have low self-esteem. Girls who are socially advanced and have verbal prowess are able to sophisticatedly verbally abuse targets, directly or indirectly, often for the amusement of others. These young people might change their behaviors if adults help them see how harmful and unfair their actions are.

Qualities Associated with Relational Aggression

Family characteristics associated with relational aggression are similar to those linked to other forms of aggression. Parents who encourage their children to respond to troublesome behaviors with aggression and who engage in aggressive behaviors themselves are prime sources of girls' aggression. Through coaching and modeling, young people learn that aggression is appropriate and even necessary to maintain order and self-respect. The types of aggression in which young people engage are those they have witnessed, experienced directly, and have seen parents and others approve and promote.

In some cases, young people only need adults to point out that their behaviors are hurtful and unjust, and they stop. Young people sometimes don't understand the consequences of their behaviors without help from others. Those who do stop typically do not have complex trauma and have not been exposed to models of aggressive behaviors over a long period of time.

When working with young people with aggressive behaviors, it is important to assess for risk and protective factors in order to plan for the kinds of interventions that might be effective with individual young people. One size does not fit all. Some young people may benefit from a brief conversation while others require relationship-building and systematic interventions.

Questions to Consider

As you think about the blog, we wonder how you are responding to the ideas we presented. We hope you consider the following questions.

* Young people learn to use relational aggression in their relationships with others. What experiences have you had that give you confidence that you as a professional can be effective in influencing young people to stop their relational aggression?

* Have you been able to engage parents when their influence on their children is harmful? In your experience, what are the conditions under which parents become engaged, change their behaviors, and the behaviors of their children become prosocial in situations that in the past led to aggression?

* Have you been able to work with school personnel who don't understand the behaviors of children in your caseload? What are the conditions under which school personnel are responsive to your concerns?

References

Crick, N. R. (1997) Engagement in gender normative versus nonnormative forms of aggression: Links to social-psychological adjustment. Developmental Psychology, 33(4), 610-617.

Crick, N.R. & Grotpeter, J.K. (1995). Relational aggression, gender, and social-psychological adjustment. Child Development, 66 (3), 710-722.

Hammel, L. R. (2008). Bouncing back after bullying: The resiliency of female victims of relational aggression. Mid-Western Educational Researcher, 21(2), 3-14.

Letendre, J. (2007). "Sugar and spice but not always nice:" Gender socialization and its impact on development and maintenance of aggression in adolescent girls. Child & Adolescent Social Work Journal. 24(4), 353-366.

Pronk, R.E. & Zimmer-Gembeck, M.J. (2010) It's "mean," but what does it mean to adolescents? Relational aggression described by victims, aggressors, and their peers. Journal of Adolescent Research. 25(2) 175-204

Blog 7

Girls' Aggression, Executive Function, and Self-Regulation

In the previous blog, we discussed the meanings of relational aggression to those who use it and factors influencing the development aggressive behaviors. In this blog, we show how notions of executive function and self-regulation can help in understanding aggression.

When girls commit relational and other forms of aggression, they are only seeing part of the picture, the part that concerns them and what they want. At the time they act, they are not considering consequences for survivors and for others, nor are they considering longer-term consequences for themselves. This is an executive function (EF) issue. Research shows that executive function is not fully developed until the mid-twenties. Many young people, whether survivors of complex trauma or not, have executive function issues. The first author has written about EF. The following is an excerpt from her book, The NEATS: A Child and Family

Assessment (Gilgun, 2011) that describes executive function.

Executive function (EF) is a term that covers a broad range of capacities related to judgment, problem-solving, organization of self, anticipation of consequences, working memory, and following rules and directions....executive functions or skills arise from a combination of genetics and experience. Adequate nutrition and good prenatal care as well as genetics lead to good executive functions at birth. Subsequent experience contributes further to executive function development. With sensitive, responsive care, children build upon existing skills to continue their optimal development.

Stress, trauma, abuse, and neglect may undermine the development of executive skills in children with a good genetic makeup. These children can recover or develop new executive skills if their circumstances change for the better and where parenting is sensitive and responsive, except if the damage to neural circuits cannot be reversed (p. 12).

Self-regulation of emotions, thought, and behaviors also are part of executive function, but in the NEATS assessment, self-regulation is so important it is treated separately. The following is a definition of self-regulation.

Self-regulation is defined as capacities to manage and make sense of one's own thoughts, emotions, and behaviors in times of stress and in the course of everyday life (Gilgun, 2011, p. 33).

The loss of capacities for self-regulation is called dysregulation. When in dysregulated states, individuals are typically reliving past trauma and are disconnected from the thinking parts of their brains, called the prefrontal cortex, where the neurological bases of executive functions reside. Persons who have experienced child abuse and neglect may have difficulties with self-regulation because parents and parental figures are likely to have been inconsistent in helping them regulate their emotions when they were infants and young children and throughout their lives. The development of self-regulation stems from the efforts of parents who help children to regulate themselves through the provision of safety, sensitivity, and contingent responsiveness. Eventually, children internalize these experiences and develop capacities for self-regulation.

Executive function, including self-regulation, are at issue when individuals act out in aggressive ways. When dysregulated, they fall back on behaviors that are deeply engrained, and they are disengaged from the thinking part of their brains. They do not consider consequences, except in a narrow way. They are unable to regulate the emotions of anger, frustration, and hurt, thoughts and beliefs that lead them to behave in aggressive ways.

Child welfare social workers have grand challenges in building relationships with girls who have issues with aggression when the girls also have problems with trust, executive function, and self-regulation. Fortunately, in many cases, girls who have aggressive behaviors seek and want trusting relationships and thus are amenable to engagement with trustworthy adults. The building of this trust may take time, and there will be setbacks. Consistency and persistence on the part of professionals often pay off.

The notions of executive function and self-regulation are helpful in understanding girls' aggression. Many people with trauma in their backgrounds develop capacities for executive function and self-regulation through the safety of secure relationships. In the next blog, we illustrate points about executive function through a case study of Antonia, a young African American girl.

As an executive function and self-regulation issue, aggression can be thought of as a form of mindlessness where persons do not consider the effects of their behaviors on others. Mindfulness, on the other hand, is living in the present moment with awareness of self, others, and the world around us. Mindfulness leads to respect, compassion, and loving-kindness toward the self, others, and all of life. Mindfulness-based practices have been used with considerable success to increase executive functions and self-regulation. We will discuss mindfulness-based interventions in blogs 8 and 9.

Questions to Consider

As you think about the blog, we wonder how you are responding to the ideas we presented. What, for example, do you think we left out? Was there anything in this blog that helped you think more deeply about your cases?

We hope you consider the following questions.

* Do you find the idea of executive function useful in your work with young people and their families? Why or why not?
* When children have secure attachments with parents and other adults, they have good executive function. Why do you think this is true?
* When children and young people are unable to self-regulate, what are your ideas about what is going on for them?
* What sense do you make of the idea that mindfulness-based practices help in fostering executive functions and capacities for self-regulation?

References

Colloroso, Barbara (2004). The bully, the bullied, and the bystander. New York: Harper Collins.

Dailey, A. L., Frey, A. J., & Walker, H. M. (2015). Relational aggression in school settings: Definition, development, strategies and implications. Children & Schools. 37(2). 79-88.

Gilgun, Jane F. (2011a). Children with serious conduct issues: A case study, a NEATS assessment, and case planning. Amazon Kindle.

Gilgun, Jane F. (2011b) The NEATS: A child & family assessment (3rd ed.). Amazon.

Lingras, K. A. (2012). For better or worse? A developmental perspective on the role of executive function in relational aggression: A dissertation submitted to the faculty of the graduate school of the University of Minnesota. University of Minnesota Libraries Digital Conservancy.

Pernice-Duca, F., Taiariol, J. & Yoon, J. (2010). Perceptions of school and family climates and experiences of relational aggression. Journal of School Violence, 100(5), 303-319

Pronk, R.E. & Zimmer-Gembeck, M.J. (2010) It's "mean," but what does it mean to adolescents? Relational aggression described by victims, aggressors, and their peers. Journal of Adolescent Research. 25(2) 175-204

Antonia: A Case Study that Illustrates Executive Function and Self-Regulation

In the previous blog, we discussed girls' aggression as executive function and self-regulation issues. In this blog, we illustrate points about executive function and self-regulation with a case study of Antonia, a young African American girl who developed prosocial behaviors through relationships of trust with a long-term case manager, with some of her teachers, and with supervisors at an after-school job.

Antonia

Antonia, a bright and attractive African-American girl, had experiences similar to many other girls in child welfare caseloads. Antonia was born to a teenage mother who rejected her at birth because Antonia was conceived through rape. Her mother placed her with aunts where Jacinta thrived. She rarely saw her mother. At five, her mother took her on what she told her aunts was an outing. Instead, the mother moved 500 miles away and took.

By this time, her mother had married and had another child whom she showered with love. Her mother not only ignored Antonia but emotionally abused her, calling her names and telling her she was the cause of her mother's problems. She also physically abused her. She and her husband often engaged in mutual verbal and physical aggression and abused drugs and alcohol. In one year, police responded 27 times to calls to the family home because of domestic abuse. Antonia saw her stepfather escorted from the home in handcuffs many times. Her mother turned in on herself at this time and did not offer comfort to Antonia. Her stepfather rarely paid attention to Antonia and sometimes physically abused her. Her favored his biological childn.

Antonia, therefore, experienced complex trauma. By age nine, her family was reported to child protection for abuse and neglect. A service provider investigated and substantiated maltreatment. Antonia's child welfare social worker provided services to the family. Antonia remained in the home. The social worker was often called to the school when Antonia was in trouble for fighting.

The child welfare service provider noticed that Antonia was able to carry on in situations where she felt safe. She had excellent verbal communication skills and did well in school and organized activities, but she had difficulty reading social cues and often verbally abused and attacked girls she thought were talking about her. She had a few girlfriends with whom she usually had amicable relationships. At times, when she felt threatened, she controlled them through threats to exclude them. The three girls sometimes engaged in relational aggression with other girls who were new to the school. Antonia enjoyed being the center of the attention and used her superior verbal skills to maintain her status. She therefore has issues with physical and relational aggression.

The child welfare social worker was concerned that Antonia would be expelled from school and follow a trajectory that would replicate her mother's life. With hope for something better for Antonia, she referred Antonia to an agency that specializes in work with children who are members of high-risk families and may be on a trajectory toward long-term anti-social behaviors and involvement in juvenile justice systems.

The program, called EXCEL (name changed) provides case management services for children from high-risk situations for as long as they are needed or up until the age of 18, whichever comes first. Antonia entered the program at age nine and continued until she was 18. She had the same case manager, whom we call Mary, for those years.

After many ups and downs, Antonia formed a trusting relationship with Mary, her case manager. Slowly, Jacinta stopped fighting other girls and thinking that they were talking about her. She appeared to stop her relational aggression. She realized that her behaviors were hurting others and herself and only made her feel worse in the long run. The case manager advocated for Antonia with teachers, school social workers, and administrators. In general, school personnel were responsive. Rather than isolating Antonia for aggressive behaviors, they allowed her to phone her case manager, which helped Antonia to calm down and return to the classroom.

School officials also allowed her to meet with the school social worker with whom she openly shared what was happening when she acted out and how her home life affected her.

School officials had a good working relationship with Mary the case manager for many years. Two teachers who specialized in children with emotional and behavioral problems were of great help to Antonia in helping her to view herself as worthy of respect and love. They applied the principles of the School-Wide Positive Behavioral Interventions and Supports (SWPBIS) that emphasizes the setting of clear expectations and the reward of prosocial behaviors.

With the recommendation and support of Mary, Antonia obtained a job in a plant nursery after school and on weekends. She excelled. At times, she became dysregulated and wanted to walk out on the job, but she phoned her case manager who helped her to re-regulate and think about consequences.

Antonia saved most of the money she earned for college and to buy clothes. She invited a classmate to her senior prom, and her case manager said she looked beautiful in the dress she bought with her own money. Her mother and stepfather allowed her to keep the money she earned, although they continued to have conflicts and also continued at times to verbally abuse and neglect Antonia.

Today, Antonia is in her second year of college, studying horticulture, in the city where her aunts live. She lives with her aunts, has close friends, and looks forward to a fulfilling future. She will require emotional support when she runs into inevitable difficulties. Hopefully, she has learned to trust others and will seek professional services for emotional support when she needs it.

The key issues that turned Antonia's life around was her long-term relationship of trust with her case manager, Mary. Mary stuck with her and listened when Antonia was troubled and dysregulated. They eventually formed a relationship of trust.

Research supports the centrality of relationships when social services have good outcomes. From all accounts, Antonia had secure attachments with her aunts and other family members from birth to the age of five. These early secure attachments are likely to have played a part in her eventual secure attachments with others. In general, when working with young people who act in aggressive ways, assessment for secure attachment experiences is important to do.

Research also has shown that factors external to service provider-service user relationships have great weight in outcome. The case manager built relationships with key school personnel who understood Antonia and helped her to deal with her self-defeating behaviors. The case manager, therefore, worked effective with external factors that otherwise might have undermined her work with Antonia.

Antonia already had good executive function and self-regulation skills when she felt safe. Building on her relationship of trust with her case manager, Antonia was able to widen her circle of trust and security to include situations where formerly she would revert to physical and relational aggression. The settings in which Antonia had good executive functions widened as her circles of trust widened.

Questions To Consider

As you think about the blog, we wonder how you are responding to the ideas we presented. What, for example, do you think we left out? Was there anything in this blog that helped you think more deeply about your cases? In addition, please consider the following questions.

* Have you been a service provider in cases similar to Antonia's? What led to the outcome?
* This case shows the centrality of relationships of trust to good outcomes. Have you noticed that your own effectiveness depends on the relationships you develop with young people and their families?
* Service providers often have to work with many other people, such as educators and parents, in order to facilitate good outcomes. Please provide examples of relationships you have had with other professionals and parents that were factors in good outcomes.

References

Appleyard, Karen, Byron Egeland, Manfred H.M. van Dulmen, and L. Alan Sroufe (2005). When more is not better: The role of cumulative risk in child behavior outcomes. Journal of Child Psychology and Psychiatry 46(3), 235–245.

Blair, Clancy, Philip David Zelazo, and Mark T. Greenberg, (2005). The measurement of executive function in early childhood. Developmental Neuropsychology. 28(2), 561–571.

Cunningham, Jera Nelson, Wendy Kliewer, & Pamelaw Garner (2009). Emotion socialization, child emotion understanding and regulation, and adjustment in urban African American families: Differential associations across child gender. Development and Psychopathology, 21, 261–283

Deater-Deckard, Kirby, Zhe Wang, Nan Chen, & Martha Ann Bell (2012). Maternal executive function, harsh parenting, and child conduct problems. Journal of Child Psychology and Psychiatry 53(10), 1084–1091.

Blog 9

Differential Assessment:
Identifying Risks and Resources

In the previous blog, we considered the case of Antonia, who at nine years old had many risks for aggressive behaviors and few resources that she was using to help her build relationships of trust that would in turn help her to cope prosocially. It took several years for Antonia to build relationships and build on her resources and to stop being aggressive. She eventually developed relationship skills to deal with stress instead of physically attacking other girls, to function well in an after-school job, to do well in school, and to gain admission to a university where she is a second-year student.

In this blog, we will present a method of differential assessment, which helps service providers to make recommendations about next steps when young people have aggressive behaviors. The purpose of differential assessment is to identify and understand the risks and resources that are present in the lives of service users and then to make recommendations for case planning based upon the risks and resources identified.

We will analyze Antonia's case, which at the beginning of service had many risks and few resources, and Christina's case, where she had many resources and few risks but she still enacted relational aggression against a long-term friend. Through these case studies, we will show how some young people change their behaviors with a minimum of services while others will require intensive services, as did Antonia.

Antonia

When Antonia became a client at ACE, she had many risks for aggressive behaviors and few easily identified protective factors. Protective factors are resources that research has associated with the development of capacities for coping with, adapting to, and overcoming risks. Examples of well-known protective factors include long-term secure attachment relationships with prosocial persons, emulation of the values, beliefs, and behaviors of these persons, good executive functions that include taking the perspectives of others, self-regulate skills that include capacities for managing emotions and behaviors, self-compassion, and compassion for others.

Antonia had many risks. Antonia's mother abducted her from the home of her aunts that Antonia remembered as loving and safe. Her mother rejected Antonia and verbally abused her, reminding her that she was a child of rape and that her mother hated the rapist. Her mother favored the younger children and told Antonia as soon as she was 18, she was out of the home. Her stepfather was indifferent to her. Her mother and stepfather engaged in verbal and physical aggression, and the police were called to their home many times. Her stepfather had a criminal record that included weapons charges, physical assault, and drug possession with intent to sell. Her mother had a history of shoplifting, writing bad checks, and physical assault. Several members of the extended family also had criminal histories that were intergenerational. Antonia's situation is typical in child welfare caseloads. It is obvious that Antonia had grown up in a high risk family. That she would believe that fighting with others girls whom she thought were making fun of her is an expectable outcome.

Antonia had some protective factors that may have been key to her eventual capacities for forming trusting relationships and her overcoming and managing her risks. The first five years of her life, according to Antonia, took place in the midst of secure, loving attachments to her aunts and their families. Antonia, like many young children with early childhood secure attachments, had an outgoing, engaging personality when she felt safe with others. Teachers reported that she was an appealing, bright, and usually well-behaved and attractive child except when she felt stressed and threatened. She did well in school but had few friends because of verbal and physical aggression.

Antonia remembers a very happy first five years. Being abducted was shocking and the long-term maternal rejection overwhelmed her capacities to cope. At nine, when she met her EXCEL case manager, Mary. It took several years for Antonia to trust Mary. It is possible that her trust of Mary built on her early experiences of secure attachment and her relationships with Mary was a factor in her trust of others and her eventual series of accomplishments.

Young people with the risks that Antonia experienced require intensive, long-term services that we will discuss in detail in later blogs.

Christina

Unlike Antonia, Christina had many long-term resources and few apparent risks. Yet, she engaged in relational aggression starting when she was in second grade. She remembers sitting at the lunch table and a new girl named Eleanor wanted to sit with Christina and her friends. Christina said, "You can't sit here. Sit somewhere else." The other girls didn't say anything. Eleanor left without a word.

These kinds of relational aggressions went unnoticed by adults until Christina was in the fifth grade when she made fun of Cynthia behind Cynthia's back and excluded Cynthia from their group of mutual friends. Cynthia had been Christina's friend since kindergarten. Cynthia got top grades, and Christina had trouble with math. Cynthia noticed that her friends began to exclude her from activities at recess and after school. One day, her teacher saw Cynthia crying at the edge of the playground and asked her what was wrong. Cynthia told her. The teacher knew that Cynthia's friends did not come from high risk situations. She also had trusting relationships with the girls.

The next day, the teacher asked the girls to stay in the classroom during recess to talk about their treatment of Cynthia. The girls said they really didn't have a reason to exclude Cynthia. The teacher said Cynthia is hurt and confused and wants to be included in her friends' activities. The girls, including Christina, felt bad.

The teacher explained how important apologies are and gave them some guidelines about how to do them. After talking to the teacher, they were eager to tell Cynthia they were sorry and to invite her back into the group. They said they didn't need the teacher's help in reaching out to Cynthia. They didn't. They apologized. Cynthia was thrilled. She was once again part of the group.

Christina had many resources and few risks. She was the third and last child in a loving family. Her older sister was married and had a family of her own. Her older brother was a star athlete on the high school basketball and baseball team and was headed for college. Both of the siblings had done well in school, and they were close to

Christina. Her mother was a loving parent who set clear rules and gave lots of praise for Christina's accomplishments. Christina shared her activities with her mother and confided in her when she was troubled. Her mother, therefore, was a secure base and a source of nurturance and love. She was also a safe haven where Cynthia could talk about things that bothered her.

Christina had one major risk factor, and that was her parents' divorce when she was five years old. The divorce came after about a year of bickering and estrangement between her parents. Christina saw her father every weekend, and he paid child support for her and her older brother. Christina felt close to her father, who took her on many outings, mostly physical activities like horseback riding, golf, and boating. She didn't talk to her father about personal things, but she enjoyed her time with him and developed confidence in her athletic abilities because of the activities they shared. She loved him and felt love from him.

The teacher knew about the divorce and thought that this could have been a factor in Christina's exclusion of Cynthia, but she could not be sure. She had a hunch that a simple intervention with Christina and her friends would be enough to change their behaviors toward Cynthia. The teacher also knew that the friends also had many resources and few risks, but not enough good judgment and sense of independence to stand up to Christina's relational aggression toward Cynthia. They simply went along with Christina.

The teacher guessed correctly that a simple intervention would work. Christina and her friends didn't realize that their behaviors were hurtful. When they thought about it, they realized that they were being unfair. They not only wanted Cynthia as their friend but they missed her and felt guilty about excluding her. They took the actions that the teacher suggested, and all was well once again.

Discussion

This kind of differential assessment is important to do so that professionals can tailor their interventions to individual cases. Medical professionals call this triage, where the type of intervention depends upon the risk and protective factors. Some young people require intensive long-term services because they have so many risks and few protective factors while others require a simple, one-time intervention and things straighten out. Simple, one-shot interventions are effective when young people have high resource and protective factors and few risks.

Questions to Consider

As you think about the blog, we wonder how you are responding to the ideas we presented. What, for example, do you think we left out? Was there anything in this blog that helped you think more deeply about your cases?

We hope you consider the following questions.

* Does differential assessment make sense to you?
* Why or why not?
* Does your agency encourage you to assess for resources and protective factors in the lives of the children and families in your caseload?
* How does the agency deliver these types of assessment?
* Do the professionals with whom you collaborate do differential assessments that focus on both risks and resources?
* If yes, how do they do these assessments?
* If no, do you have any reasons to wish that they did?

References

Gilgun, Jane F. (2013). Resilience is relational. Amazon.

Gilgun, Jane F. (2006). Children and adolescents with problematic sexual behaviors: Lessons from research on resilience. In Robert Longo & Dave Prescott (Eds.), Current perspectives on working with sexually aggressive youth and youth with sexual behavior problems (pp. 383-394). Holyoke, MA: Neari Press.

Hughes, Karen (2012). The roots of resilience. Nature, 490 (October), 165-167.

Masten, Ann S. (2014). Ordinary magic: Resilience in development. New York: Guilford.

Unger, Michael & Linda Liebengerg (2008). Resilience in action: Working with youth across cultures and contexts. Toronto: University of Toronto.

Blog 10

Relational Interviews
and Relationship-Based Interventions

Summary

Most people think that when girls are aggressive, they must be punished. In this blog, we describe how to build relationships with girls who act in aggressive ways. This requires one-on-one conversations where an adult asks open-ended questions. Adults listen and say little. The purpose is to get to know the girls and what their aggression means to them. Trust develops. The girls are surprised that an adult takes the time to try to understand them and get to know them. Building relationships through one-on-one conversations is the beginning of effective work.

Relationship-Based Interventions

Our primary focus is on relationship-based interventions. We chose relationship-based interventions for four reasons.

1. Research on attachment shows that individuals who have secure attachment relationships, which by definition are based on trust, engage in prosocial behaviors and have good executive function and self-regulation skills.

2. Social work has long held that effective practice is based on relationships. More than 50 years ago, Helen Harris Perlman taught that relationship based on trust are the foundations of empathy, warmth, and safety that service users require for them to identify and work through issues associated with problematic situations.

3. An accumulation of research evidence that shows relationships are the second most important factor in social services outcomes.

4. Research has shown that external factors have the largest
influence on outcome. There are systems issues. Research also shows that changing problematic systems

begins with building relationships with persons who compose these systems. Only through relationships are systems changes possible.

We begin our discussion of relationship-based interventions with descriptions of procedures that lead to positive outcomes. The procedures themselves can become stand-alone interventions or they can be adapted to work within other programs.

Relational Interviews

We recommend that work with young people with aggressive behaviors begin with one-on-one conversations called relational interviews. These conversations take place when young people are in regulated states; that is, when they are in a calm state and not stressed and dysregulated. The purposes of the interviews are to encourage persons to talk about what matters to them. In doing so, relationships of trust develop.

Those conducting the interviews have skills in asking open-ended questions, have active listening skills, and capacities for empathy while at the same time they maintain their own analytic stances. Principals, vice principals, school counselors, school social workers, mentors, child protection social workers, and other service providers are candidates for engaging young people in relational interviews.

The interviews are based on open-ended questions, take place in private settings, and are non-coercive. Non-coercion means interviewers inform young people that they do not have to answer any questions they do not want to. Interviewers understand the line between respect for privacy and desire to get to know other persons.

The interview begins with open-ended questions that ask young people about activities they enjoy. Examples are "How's it going?" "What kinds of things did you do over the weekend?" "How did you learn to dance so well?" or some other question that asks young people to talk about something that is meaningful to them. These conversations can be relatively brief.

Moving into issues related to aggression requires a period of transition, where adults can tell young people what the purpose of the meeting is. The following is an example, "A few days ago, you got into it with other students. I'm wondering what was going on for you."

Then interviewers listen. Examples of other open-ended questions are "What was going on for you when you told Alicia she couldn't sit with you? [or posted comments about Maddie on the internet/told your friends not to invite Celia to the overnight?"]

Follow up questions depend upon what the young people say but the kinds of questions that might be helpful are "What do you think about this now?" "Have you seen other people do this?" "Has this been done to you?" "What did you hope to get out of these behaviors?" "Have you thought about how the other person might feel?" "What do you think other people are feeling?" What questions to ask, comments to make, and the timing of questions and comments are a matter of judgment.

Well-done interviews are contingently responsive, meaning that interviewers are attuned to the girls and interact in ways that keep them connected to what is happening for the girls. When relationships are contingently responsive, people feel accepted and understood. Relationship-based social work and attachment theory have long shown that feeling accepted and understood has many benefits. Among them are self-compassion, compassion for others, awareness of the effects of one's behaviors on others, and mindfulness.

Relational Interviews and Listening

In relational interviews, adults listen and say little. Through such interviews, adults discover not only what the behaviors mean to young people but also the beliefs and emotions that lead to the behaviors. In the course of showing interest, not judging, and listening well, adults provide a safe haven for the young people who may slowly begin to trust the adults.

These trusting relationships then become the basis of further work with the young people, such as drawing them into more formalized group interventions and providing guidance for how to conduct themselves in situations that trouble them.

Questions to Consider

As you think about the blog, we wonder how you are responding to the ideas we presented. What, for example, do you think we left out? Was there anything in this blog that helped you think more deeply about your cases?

* Do you see possibilities that relational interviews might be helpful to you in your work?
* Do you see how attachment theory is part of relational interviews? For example, contingent responsiveness, safe havens, and trust are important concepts in attachment theory. How helpful do you think relational interviews and attachment theory are to your work?

References

Brown, Kirk Warren, Richard M. Ryan and J. David Creswell (2007). Mindfulness: Theoretical foundations and evidence for its salutary effects. Psychological Inquiry 18 (4), 211-237.

Cameron, Mark, & Elizabeth King Keenan (2010). The common factors model: Implications for transtheoretical clinical social work practice. Social Work, 55(1), 63-73.

Drisko, James W. (2004). Common factors in psychotherapy outcome. Families in Society, 85 (1), 81-90.

Fonagy, Peter, George Gergely, & Mary Target (2007). The parent–infant dyad and the construction of the subjective self. Journal of Child Psychology and Psychiatry 48 (3/4), 288–328.

Gecan, Michael (). Going public. Boston: Beacon.

Gilgun, Jane F. (2011). Children with serious conduct issues: A case study, a NEATS assessment, and case planning. Amazon Kindle.

Lambert, M. (1992). Implications of outcome research for psychotherapy integration. In J. Norcross & J. Goldstein (Eds.), Handbook of psychotherapy integration (pp. 94-129) NY: Basic.

Mullet, Judy Hostetler (2014). Restorative discipline: From getting even to getting well. Children & Schools, 36 (3), 157-162.

Perlman, Helen Harris (1957). Social casework: A problem-solving process. Chicago: University of Chicago.

Blog 11

Group Work
and Relationship-Based Practice

In the previous blog, we discussed principles of relationship-based practice and relational interviews as preparation for young people to transition into group work. In this blog, we propose an approach to group work that builds on relationship-based practice and relational interviews. Through effective group work, young people widen their circles of trust and develop relationship skills and skills in executive function and self-regulation. They become more aware of the effects of their behaviors on others and develop mindfulness.

Group Work

Once professionals have developed relationships of trust with young people, they can begin to invite girls to participate in group work. The group would be composed of five to six girls and two adults, at least one of whom has participated in relational interviews with each girl. One or both of the leaders would be knowledgeable about methods of self-regulation, such as guided imagery, breathing exercises along the lines of "smell the rose and blow out the candle," meditation, yoga, tai chi, and other relaxation practices. If those who conducted the relational interviews don't have this kind of training, they can invite a person who does to co-lead or teach the skills on an as-needed basis. The group would be time-limited with four sessions and the option to renew participation for another four weeks.

Goals

The goals of the group are to grow relationships of trust and to develop skills in self-regulation. Given the limited time that professionals often have for group work, these goals may have to be enough. Service providers can hope and work toward other goals. These goals include

* to go beyond individualized methods self-regulation such as breathing exercises, and to develop capacities to seek trusted others in times of stress to avert engaging in aggressive or other harmful behaviors;
* to enhance executive function, such as anticipation of consequences, planning for the future, self-organization, understanding social norms, and following rules;

* Repair of relationships that their aggression has harmed would be another goal;

* through relationships to develop compassion for self and others; and

* to develop mindfulness so that they have capacities to be attuned to their own inner states and the inner states of others and to act with respect toward the self and others.

These goals provide a vision for best possible outcomes. In practice, service providers know that reaching even some of these goals would mark success. In school settings and in situations where child welfare social workers have long-term relationships, these goals can provide guidelines for everyday interactions with clients in order to foster the development of prosocial behaviors. When they interact with young people, these goals can help them decide what to say and do.

The four-week group experience may be the foundation for further participation in group work and other interventions, such as those based on the principles of restorative justice. We will discuss specific programs in the final blog.

Voluntary Participation

Participation in the group is voluntary. Groups would be about an hour long. Each session would open with a check in and a brief guided mediation on something pleasant, such as going for a massage or a swim in a warm lagoon loaded with colorful fish. If the girls are anxious or dysregulated at check-in, the guided imagery may help the girls to re-regulate.

In the group, the girls share with each other the kinds of issues they discussed in the relational interviews. This discussion will be wide-ranging because aggression has multiple meanings and sources. Group facilitators will notice when girls become emotional and appear to be on the verge of dysregulation. They will then lead groups into exercises helpful for re-regulation.

Guided meditation, guided imagery, naming a quality they admire in a person they know, sharing a time when they had done something that others appreciated, or when someone had done something they appreciated are ways to help young people re-regulate. Something as simple as breathing exercises taught with the guideline of "Smell the rose, and put out the candle" is helpful to many

(Danette Jones, personal communication, February 2015).

Homework assignments would include practicing what they learn in their group work at least one time per week and be prepared to report on how they did at check-in at the beginning of the next group. Facilitators would not pressure the girls into doing these assignments. They would simply make suggestions and at the next group inquire about whether they got to doing the assignment.

Self-Determination

Sometimes facilitators guide the discussion with questions based on principles of repair of relationships that their aggression has harmed. A question that might open up this possibility is "Would you like to make it right?" Some girls may not think they do. Instead, they might launch into a justification of their violence. Group facilitators would view a pro-violence stance as the girls' right to choose, or their right to self-determination. They might even be encouraged that the girls are putting their beliefs out in the open. When this happens, group leaders would give the young person the time and space to hear her own beliefs in a safe environment. In the best case, the group work would result in young people hearing many points of view about violence. They may begin to want to chose other ways of dealing with troublesome situations.

The only way they will change is when they are ready and willing. They may want to learn how to repair relationships. This includes taking responsibility for the actions, understanding what was going on for themselves at the time, understanding the effects of their behaviors on others, and wanting to engage in prosocial behaviors. They would be willing to meet with the person or persons they've harmed, be willing to listen to what others say is the effects of their aggression, and be willing to apologize.

Apologies take time to compose and practice. Preparation for repair may not be possible in a four-week group and not even in an eight-week group. The repair of specific relationships may take place after the group experience and in a restorative justice program that we discuss in the final blog.

Inviting Others In

During the last 15 minutes of each group, parents, teachers, and other school staff would be invited to join the girls so that the girls could share with them what they discussed and learned in group. It is important to include as many other people in the girls' group work so that people in the wider settings can be supportive.

Evaluation

Evaluation of the effects of the group would be on-going, beginning with group facilitators noticing how the girls interact in group, what the girls say about the effects, how the girls behave in other settings, and what others say about the girls' behaviors in other setting. Group facilitators would meet beforehand to plan the group and would meet after each group to discuss what happened in the group and to begin to plan for the following group.

Self-Compassion

Self-compassion is a possible consequence of group work. As stated in Blog 1, persons who have self-compassion accept themselves as imperfect and hold themselves accountable for any hurt they cause. They seek to repair damage to relationship with others. If persons have self-compassion, they have compassion for others. Their compassion for others and themselves flows from an inner sense of dignity and self-worth.

Research shows that low self-compassion is associated with harsh experiences, usually in childhood and sometimes later in life, and the absence of relationships with others that provide safe havens where individuals can work through the effects of these experiences. Child abuse and neglect, rape, separations and losses, and other adverse and traumatic events are examples of harsh experiences. Girls with child protection involvement have lower self-compassion. Research shows that they are more likely to engage in aggressive behaviors and to be targets of aggression than girls without child protection involvement. Research shows self-compassion can be increased through positive life experiences based on relationships of trust.

Summary

In summary, over the four sessions, participants would form relationships of trust, share beliefs and meanings about violence, learn methods of self-regulation, be exposed to ideas regarding repair of relationships, and hopefully develop self-compassion and compassion for others.

Some girls may want to continue for another four weeks. The structure of the group would remain the same. The girls would have a lot to share. Four additional weeks would deepen and broaden their capacities for relationships of trust, self-regulation, executive function, self-compassion, and compassion for others.

These are big goals that are unlikely to be achieved in four weeks or eight weeks. Relational interviews and relationship-based group work might be a solid beginning. Girls may begin to seek out people they trust, as Antonia did after developing a long-term relationship of trust with her case manager. (See Blog 8 on Antonia's case.)

Questions to Consider

If you think we've left something out, please let us know. If this blog has given you something to think about, we'd like to know your thoughts. Please consider the following questions.

* Group work has a long history in social work. What experiences have you had in group work? For example,

o Have you ever participated in group work? If yes, what was your experience?

o Have you had formal or informal training in group work? What kind of training did you have? Have you found it useful in your practice?

o Have you ever developed a group intervention? What was your experience?

o Have you ever facilitated a group? What was your experience?

* How do the idea in this blog fit with your understandings of group work with children and young people? For example, what do you think of self-compassion as a goal of group work?

References

Brown, Kirk Warren, Richard M. Ryan and J. David Creswell (2007). Mindfulness: Theoretical foundations and evidence for its salutary effects. Psychological Inquiry 18 (4), 211-237.

Comer E, Meier, A. & Galinsky, M.J. (2004) Development of innovative group work practice using the intervention research paradigm. Social Work 49(2), 250–260.

Mullet, Judy Hostetler (2014). Restorative discipline: From getting even to getting well. Children & Schools, 36 (3), 157-162.

Moore, Monique, David Brown, Nisha b, & Mark Bates (2011). Mind body skills for regulating the autonomic nervous system. Arlington, VA: Defense centers of excellence for psychological health and traumatic brain injury.

Neff, K. D. & McGehee, P. (2010). Self-compassion and psychological resilience among adolescents and young adults. Self and Identify, 9(3), 225–240.

Pargament, Kenneth I. (2007). Spiritually integrated psychotherapy. New York: Guilford.

Blog 12

Relationship-Based
Intervention Programs

There are many interventions programs for children with aggression issues. Some are school-based, some involve both schools and families, and some are primarily family-based. Some make efforts to address issues of racial disproportionality, but, for the most part, this remains an issue that goes largely unaddressed. Many of them are school-wide programs and others target young people who have issues with aggression. Some of the interventions we discuss in this blog are well-evaluated systematic programs, while others are approaches intended to increase self-awareness, awareness of others, self-regulation, and executive functions.

Child protection workers who are familiar with these programs and approaches are positioned to make recommendations to school personnel about programs that fit work within their particular settings. We describe several of these programs. Each of them is based on at least some of the principles we have discussed earlier in this series of blogs.

Preventing Relational Aggression
In Schools Everyday (PRAISE)

PRAISE is a school-based intervention that addresses relational aggression in urban areas. Implemented school-wide, PRAISE is a universal prevention program that does not single out particular students, thus reducing the possibility of stigmatization. PRAISE is delivered in 20 sessions, lead by therapists and a classroom teacher. The program consists of role plays, videos, and culturally adapted cartoons to raise awareness of the nature of relational aggression and its consequences. The program is for both aggressors and targets of relational aggression. Some young people engage in both roles, as discussed earlier.

Evaluations show that the program is effective for girls but not for boys. Girls show increased knowledge of relational aggression and increased capacities for anger management and the processing of social information. Also, participation in the program reduces girls incidence of relational aggression. PRAISE had no such effects for boys.

School-Wide Positive Behavioral Interventions and Supports (SWPBIS)

SWPBIS is a program that has been implemented in 16,000 schools in the United States. The program sets clear expectations and rewards prosocial behaviors. Evaluations show that the program increases students' sense of safety in schools and reduces acts of aggression. The model is three-tired. The first tier is a school-wide intervention where school staff teach students definitions of types of behaviors and set expectations. Through tracking incidence of acts of aggression, school staff identify students who would benefit from more targeted interventions. These interventions include teaching skills targeting self-regulation, the development of friendships, and conflict resolution. The most intensive level of interventions involves work with parents and teachers to develop strategies for dealing with aggressive and disruptive behaviors.

Boneshefski and Rung (2014) have suggestions for how school personnel can identify whether disciplinary practices result in racial disproportionality. If disproportionality is found to exist, the authors suggest ways of identifying the behaviors that lead to disproportionality. They include observations of interactions between students and teachers, teacher surveys, and self-study for school personnel.

Families and Schools Together (FAST)

FAST is an eight-week to ten-week program for parents and children from three age groups: elementary, middle school, and high school. For each age level, parents and children engage in activities together, parents have activities with other parents, and children have activities with other children. The intervention takes place in multiple-family groups of about ten children and families with group leaders who are representative of the populations and settings that are served. The team of leaders are teachers, parents, and community-based professionals. Teenagers are part of the leadership team for the middle- and high-school groups. The ethnicity of team leaders is consistent with the ethnicity of program participants. Each team leader receives intensive training and certification. Once the eight to ten week part of the program ends, parents meeting weekly for two years.

The purposes of FAST are to build parent-child relationships, to provide parents with ideas and skills that they use to help their children develop social and self-regulation skills, improve school climate, and build relationships between parents who often are otherwise isolated. Research show that FAST is an effective intervention that has a high rate of success in meeting program goals. Further information about FAST is available on the internet and through evaluation of reports, such as (Guerra & Knox, 2008). McDonald et al, 2012).

Interventions to Increase Executive Function and Self-Regulation

Since aggressive behaviors are associated with belief systems and difficulties with capacities for self-regulation and executive function, it makes sense to teach children ways to become aware of their beliefs, the consequences of their beliefs, and how to regulate their emotions, thoughts, and behaviors. Mindfulness-based practice, yoga, and meditation can do that. In fact, they are increasingly part of school curricula. School social workers and child protection workers who want to initiate such programs into schools either required specialized training themselves or have funding to hire specialists.

Examples of interventions that can increase executive function and self-regulation include computerized training for executive skills, aerobic exercises that have been show to increase executive functions, martial arts, mindfulness-based practices, yoga, meditation, and music and dance therapy. Research shows that combinations of these activities are more effective than any one individual activity.

Research shows that mindfulness-based interventions are associated with increases in self-compassion and compassion for others in adult and in high school students. These findings are based on programs for adults. At present, school-based programs appear not to have been evaluated regarding impact on self-compassion and compassion for others.

Restorative Justice

Restorative justice is a growing national and international movement that brings survivors and perpetrators together for the purpose of healing the hurt and repairing relationships that aggression and violence have harmed. Victims, offenders, and persons important to victims and offenders come together to find solutions that include accountability and that promote healing and reconciliation. Restorative justice represents a shift from punishment to reconciliation and gives opportunities for survivors to tell perpetrators what their behaviors mean to them. Other persons affected, such as family members and friends also have such opportunities.

Trained service providers spend as much time as necessary to prepare persons for restorative justice dialogues. Some perpetrators, survivors, families, and friend decline to participate, but those who do report its benefits. Restorative justice is a promising response to punitive and ineffective policies that we discussed in the first three blogs in this series.

Restorative justice programs are a grown trend in schools. They require extensive training of school staff, students, and parents. A recent evaluation concluded that good outcomes depend upon a goodness of fit between the settings and the programs. After reviewing research on school-based restorative justice programs Armour (2013) and Gonzalez (2012) concluded that they have disrupt the school to prison pipeline.

Summary

There are many well-evaluated school-based programs that are effective in reducing incidence of aggression and fostering increased self-regulation and executive functions. In addition, there are promising approaches such as meditation, yoga, physical exercise, and martial arts whose research based suggest effectiveness as well. Restorative justice programs, too, have increasing levels of documentation that show that they are effective as well.

These interventions are based upon many of the principles we discussed in this blog series, such as the centrality of relationships and the importance self-regulation, executive function, self-compassion, and compassion.

Questions to Consider

If you think we've left something out, please let us know. If this blog has given you something to think about, we'd like to know your thoughts. Please consider the following questions.

* For programs to be effective there must be a goodness of fit between programs and settings. Do you agree with this statement or have a some disagreements? Why or why not?
* How feasible do you think the programs discussed in this blog are for schools in which you as child welfare social workers collaborate? What might facilitate the effective implementation of these programs and what might get in the way?
* Can you name other programs that you know from experience work well in school settings? What are they? Why do you think they work?

References

Armour, M. (2013). Ed White Middle School restorative discipline evaluation: Implementation and impact, 2012/2013, sixth grade. Retrieved from the

University of Texas at Austin, Institute for Restorative Justice and Restorative Dialogue. http://www.utexas.edu/research/cswr/rji/pdf/Ed_White_Evaluation2012-2013.pdf. Retrieved August 16, 2015.

Blair, Clancy & C. Cybele Raver (2014). Closing the achievement gap through modification of neurocognitive and neuroendocrine function: Results from a cluster randomized controlled trial of an innovative approach to the education of children in kindergarten. Plos One, 9(11), 1-13.

Boneshefski, Michael J. & Timothy J. Rung (2014). Addressing disproportionate discipline practices within a School-Wide Positive Behavioral Interventions and Supports framework: A practical guide for calculating and using disproportionality rates. Journal of Positive Behavior Interventions, 16(3), 149–158.

Conduct Problems Prevention Research Group (2010). Universal social–emotional learning program: The role of student and school characteristics. Journal of Consulting and Clinical Psychology, 78, 156–168.

Diamond, Adele (2013). Executive functions. Annual Review of Psychology, 64, 135-168.

Dymnicki, Allison B., Roger P. Weissberg, & David B. Henry (2011). Understanding how programs work to prevent overt aggressive behaviors: A meta-analysis of mediators of elementary school-based programs. Journal of School Violence, 10(4), 315-337.

Flook, Lisa, Susan M. Smalley, M. Jennifer Kittel, Brian M. Gala, Susan Kaiser-Greenland, Jill Locke, Eric Ishijima, & Connie Kasari (2010). Effects of mindful awareness practices on executive functions in elementary school children. Journal of Applied Psychology, 26, 70-95.

Gonzalez, Thalia (2012). Keeping kids in schools: Restorative justice, punitive discipline, and the school to prison pipeline. Journal of Law and Education, 41(2), 281-335.

Guerra, Nancy & Lindee Knox (2008). How culture impacts the dissemination and implementation of innovation: A case study of the Families and Schools Together Program (FAST) for preventing violence with immigrant Latino youth. American Journal of Community Psychology, 41(3), 304-313.

Hahn, R., Fuqua-Whitley, D., Wethington, H., Lowy, J., Liberman, A., Crosby, A., et al. (2007). The effectiveness of universal school-based programs to prevent violent and aggressive behavior: A systematic review. American Journal of Preventive Medicine, 33, S114–S129.

Hendry, R. (2009). Building and restoring respectful relationships in schools. New York: Routledge.

Horner, Robert H., George Sugai, & Cynthia M. Anderson (2010) Examining the evidence base for school-side positive behavior support. Focus on Exceptional Children, 42(8), 1-11.

Leff, Stephen. S. & Nicki R. Crick. (2010). Interventions for relational aggression: Innovative programming and next steps in research and practice. School Psychology Review. 39(4), 504-507.

Leff, Stephen. S., Tracy Evian Waasdorp, Brooke Paskewich, Rebecca Laken Gullan, Abbas F. Jawad, Julie Paquette MacEvoy, Betsy E. Feinberg, & Thomas J. Power (2010). The Preventing Relational Aggression in Schools Everyday Program: A preliminary evaluation of acceptability and impact. School Psychology Review, 39, 569–587.

McDonald, Lynn, Sarah Fitzroy, Irene Fuchs, Insa Fooken, & Henrikje Klasen (2012). Strategies for high retention rates in low-income families in FAST (Families and Schools Together): An evidence-based parenting programme in the US, UK, Holland, and Germany. European Journal of Developmental Psychology 9(1), 75-88.

Moore, Monique, David Brown, Nisha b, & Mark Bates (2011). Mind body skills for regulating the autonomic nervous system. Arlington, VA: Defense centers of excellence for psychological health and traumatic brain injury.

Mullet, Judy Hostetler (2014). Restorative discipline: From getting even to getting well. Children & Schools, 36 (3), 157-162.

Riestenberg, N. (2012). Circle in the square: Building community and repairing harm in school. St. Paul, MN: Living Justice Press.

Sumner, M. D., Silverman, C. J., & Frampton, M. L. (2010). School-based restorative justice as an alternative to zero-tolerance policies: Lessons from West Oakland (pp. 1-36). University of California, Berkeley: Thelton E Henderson Center for Social Justice.

Umbreit, Mark & Marilyn Armour (2010). Restorative dialogue: An essential guide for research and practice. New York: Springer.

Zoogman, Sarah, Simon B. Goldber, William T. Hoyt & Lisa Miller (2015). Mindfulness interventions with youth: A meta-analysis. Mindfulness, 6, 290–302

Blog 13

Systems Change
Through Relationship-Based Interviews

In previous blogs, we discussed relational interviews as a means of getting to know young people and building circles of trust. In this blog, we show how relational interviews can create change in systems that are punitive when young people act in aggressive ways.

Systems Change

Child protection social workers know through experience that school authorities have policies and procedures for dealing with students who behave in aggressive ways. Many schools have zero-tolerance or close to zero-tolerance policies where students are punished immediately for any infraction that authorities believe threatens safety. This may solve the immediate problem by getting the troublesome student out of the setting, but long-term issues remain. Mullet (2014) reported that a principal told her "I know that punishment doesn't really change the student, but at least everyone involved knows that I did something" (p. 157). Not only does punishment not help but it can become part of a sequences of negative consequences that we have discussed in previous blogs.

Child welfare social workers have roles to play in changing ineffective policies, procedures, and programs. Principals, teachers, and other school staff often have engrained beliefs such as punishment is an appropriate response. At the same time, they typically have an inkling that punishment doesn't work in the long run.

Organizing for Relational Interviews

Child welfare social workers can initiate a series of relational interviews with parents, school social workers, guidance counselors, and school staff. They may find among them persons who want to join them to plan for systems change. Those conducting the interviews would have the necessary skills as described earlier, and the principle of non-coercion would be in play.

Interviewers would ask parents about their children, what they think of school policies, and whether they would like to see school policies change. As interviewers build relationships with parents, they could invite parents to meet in small groups to discuss concerns. Through these meetings, parents may form coalitions and make plans for meeting with administrators, teachers, staff such as janitors, teachers' aides, and lunch room servers, and school boards to discuss current policies and programs and changes they would like to see. Interviewers would become "background facilitators," present and available for consultation and supportive of the emergence of parent leaders.

Services to Parents

Through building relationships with parents, interviewers may learn about the roles of families in the aggressive behaviors. Interviewers would have relationships with parents and information on which to make recommendations for parents about what to do for their children. This could include referrals to parent support groups, self-help groups such as those based on the 12 Steps, and individual and family therapy. Job preparation and training, educational programs, recreation, and any other resources would be opportunities interviewers could offer parents.

In informational interviews with school personnel, interviewers would inquire about the reasoning and meanings behind current policies and guide conversations toward the effectiveness and consequences of current practices. Naturally or with a bit of encouragement, school officials might begin to wonder out loud about what might be more effective.

Interviewers could make gentle suggestions about principles and programs that have been shown to be effective. Slowly and carefully, relational interviews can change views about how to deal with children and young people who have issues with aggression.

Well-done interviews are contingently responsive, meaning that interviewers are attuned to school officials and staff. They interact in ways that keep them connected to what is happening for the people they interview.

Partnering with Parents for Systems Change

Interviewers could work toward getting parents and school staff to work together to change policies and to initiate new approaches to children and young people who behave in aggressive ways.

Interviewers could also approach school board members. Relational interviews with them could lead to changes in school districts. If the work parents and school personnel have done together has gone well, they could conduct the relational interviews with members of school boards. These interviews would build coalitions that could result in district-wide changes in policies and programs.

Such movements toward systems changes have a chance of being effective with careful planning and evaluations after each step. Based on evaluations of what has already happening, child protection social workers and the growing number of parent and school allies could work toward program and polices research and practice experience have shown to be effective.

Summary

In summary, individual and systems change happens through relationships of trust. Child protection social workers have leadership roles to play with parents who might want to see changes in school policies and who also might realize that they have to change their own behaviors for the sake of their children and for their own sakes.

Child protection social workers, especially if they can collaborate with parent groups, may be catalysts for change in schools and other settings. Relational interviews with young people can build communities of support, where young people have persons to whom they can turn when they are about to act out in aggressive ways. Finally, the people who compose the systems that affect young people often are frustrated with the results of their policies. Relational interviews with them can explore these issues and lead to systems changes.

Questions To Consider

As you think about the blog, we wonder how you are responding to the ideas we presented.

* What do you think of relational interviews as a way of creating systems change?
* Can you picture yourself doing relational interviews for systems change? Why or why not?
* Can you picture yourself organizing others, such as other child protection social workers, school social

workers, guidance counselors, and teachers to do relationship interviews?

* What would be involved in leading such an effort?

References

Brown, Kirk Warren, Richard M. Ryan and J. David Creswell (2007). Mindfulness: Theoretical foundations and evidence for its salutary effects. Psychological Inquiry 18 (4), 211-237.

Gecan, Michael (). Going public. Boston: Beacon.

Gilgun, Jane F. (2011). Children with serious conduct issues: A case study, a NEATS assessment, and case planning. Amazon Kindle.

Hoglund, W. L., & Leadbeater, B. J. (2004). The effects of family, school, and class- room ecologies on changes in children's social competence and emotional and behavioral problems in first grade. Developmental Psychology, 40, 533–544.

Kahn, Si (2010). Creative community organizing. San Francisco: Berret-Koehler.

Mullet, Judy Hostetler (2014). Restorative discipline: From getting even to getting well. Children & Schools, 36 (3), 157-162.

Neff, K. D. & McGehee, P. (2010). Self-compassion and psychological resilience among adolescents and young adults. Self and Identify, 9(3), 225–240.

Rubin, Herbert J. & Irene Rubin (2008). Community organizing and development (4th ed.). New York: Pearson.

About the Authors

JANE F. GILGUN, Ph.D., LICSW, is a professor, School of Social Work, University of Minnesota, Twin Cities, USA. She was a child welfare social worker for more than eight years and has taught courses and done qualitative research on high-risk children and families for many years. A special focus of her research is factors associated with good outcomes when children have experienced complex trauma. Professor Gilgun's articles, books, and practice manuals are widely available on the internet. Many of them are free.

SAMANTHA HIRSCHEY, MSW, LSW, WAS a master's student at the School of Social Work, University of Minnesota, USA, and Professor Gilgun's research assistant at the time of the writing of these blogs. She did her first year internship at the St. Paul Public Schools and her second internship will be at the Community-University Health Care Center that provides mental health services to residents of the inner city of Minneapolis. She has worked in a variety of social service agencies including with children, teens, and adults with mental illnesses and developmental disabilities. She has a special interest in the promotion of integrated behavioral health in children and families.

This series was first published by the Center for Advanced Studies in Child Welfare (CASCW, http://cascw.umn.edu), School of Social Work, College of Education and Human Development, University of Minnesota, Twin Cities, USA, with support, in part, by grant #GRK%80888 from the Minnesota Department of Human Services, Children and Family Services Division, by the Minnesota Agricultural Experiment Station Grant 55-064, and Ramsey County Community Human Services, Minnesota, USA, September 2015.

www.ingramcontent.com/pod-product-compliance
Lightning Source LLC
Chambersburg PA
CBHW071154280526
45787CB00002B/503